SharePoint 2013 Survey Ramp-Up Guide

STEVEN MANN

SharePoint 2013 Survey Ramp-Up Guide

Copyright © 2014 by Steven Mann

Trademarks

Screenshots of Microsoft Products and Services

Warning and Disclaimer

Introduction

This guide steps users through the creation and use of surveys in SharePoint. It is geared towards new users of both SharePoint 2013 and Surveys in SharePoint. Using the guide, users will understand various aspects of working with surveys in SharePoint 2013:

- Planning a Survey
- Adding a Survey to a Site
- Creating Free Form Questions
- Creating Choice Questions
- Configuring Rating Scale Questions
- Creating and Configuring Branching Questions
- Adding Page Separators
- Reordering Questions
- Configuring Survey Options
- Configuring Response Permissions
- Managing Survey Responses

Survey Overview

You may easily create surveys in SharePoint to solicit feedback for various business purposes anywhere from employee satisfaction to holiday party planning. Creating a survey in SharePoint involves adding a Survey app to one of your sites.

Essentially, as with many things in SharePoint, a survey is a glorified list of survey responses with the columns being the actual questions. However with these questions come special types such as the Rating Scale as well as special survey functionality such as branching and page separators.

Anyone can dive right in and fumble with the question creation and branching but to generate a decent survey the first time around without too much fumbling and re-work, it is best to plan out your survey questions first while understanding the various types of user inputs available.

Planning Your Survey Questions

Planning your survey questions involves both what feedback you are trying to obtain along with how it should be obtained. This correlates with the question/answer entry types that are available in SharePoint along with how the responses are presented. This section lists examples of the common types that should be used in a survey and may be used as a guide to help you decide what type of answer is appropriate for your questions.

Free Form Single Entry

A free form single entry may be used to ask a question that may have many possible answers but not finite enough to provide choices. This is where you want the user to enter whatever they feel without being constrained to a list of choices.

User Entry Interface

What is your favorite color?

Blue

Graphical Response Summary

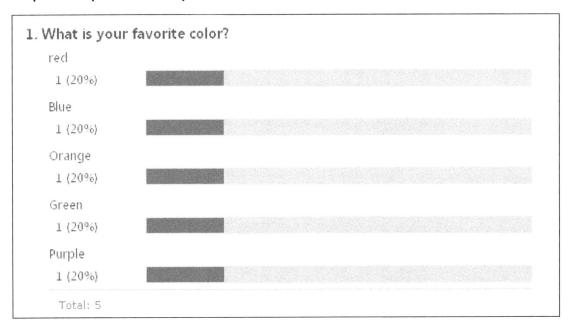

Free Form Multiple Line

A free form multiple line entry should be used when you would like the user to describe an issue or problem, provide a relatively longer (than the single line) explanation , expand on comments, or provide recommendations/suggestions.

User Entry Interface

Please describe your main responsibilities: *

I am involved in creating solutions on our intranet that runs on SharePoint 2013.

Graphical Response Summary

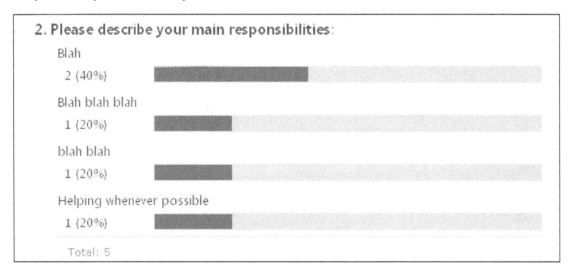

Choice Question as Drop-Down

A choice question allows you to enter specific choices in which the user may select as the answer. For the drop-down type, the choices appear in a drop-down list. This type of answer interface is good for questions that may have several possible selections (5-10) but obviously works with two or more.

User Entry Interface

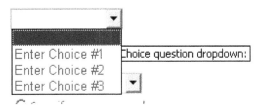

Graphical Response Summary

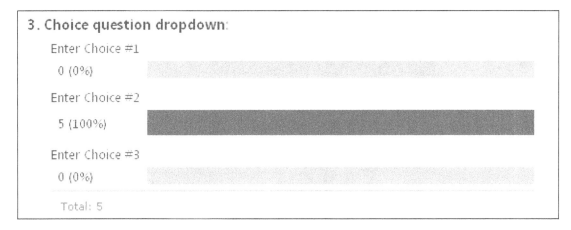

Choice Question as Drop-Down with Fill-In

Using the optional "Allow Fill-In" selection allows you to create a question that provides both a drop-down menu and an option for the user to enter their own answer.

If you are going to allow the user to fill-in their own answer, using the options or the checkboxes (explained in the next sub-sections) provides a more naturally mapped user interface.

User Entry Interface

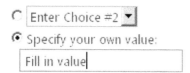

Graphical Response Summary

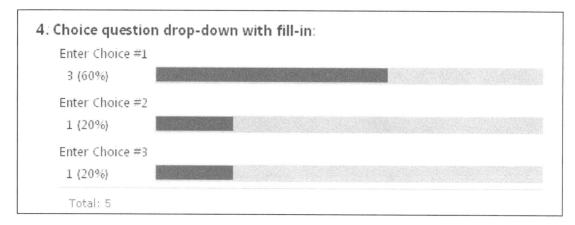

Choice Question as Options (Radio Buttons)

For the Options type of choice question, the available answers to the question are presented as radio buttons in which only one may be selected. This is similar to the drop-down menu however, the user can see all options available without having the look inside the drop-down.

User Entry Interface

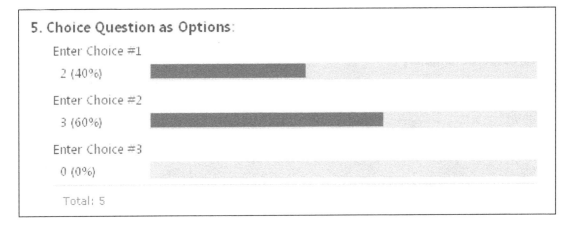

Graphical Response Summary

Choice Question as Options (Radio Buttons) with Fill-In

Using the optional "Allow Fill-In" selection allows you to create a question that provides both pre-defined options along with an option for the user to enter their own answer.

If you are going to allow the user to fill-in their own answer, using the options as shown here provides a more naturally mapped user interface (versus with the drop-down menu).

User Entry Interface

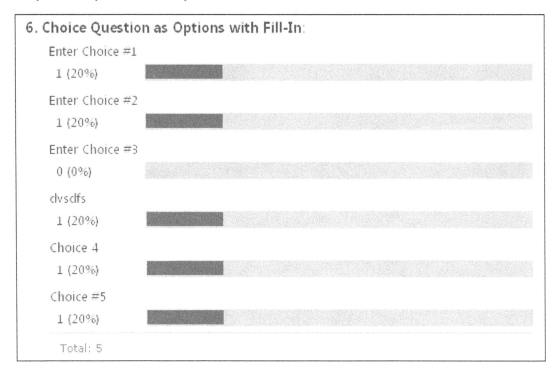

Graphical Response Summary

6. Choice Question as Options with Fill-In:

Enter Choice #1
1 (20%)

Enter Choice #2
1 (20%)

Enter Choice #3
0 (0%)

dvsdfs
1 (20%)

Choice 4
1 (20%)

Choice #5
1 (20%)

Total: 5

Choice Question with Checkboxes (Multiple Selection)

For the Checkboxes type of choice question, the available answers to the question are presented as checkboxes in which the user may select one or more answers.

User Entry Interface

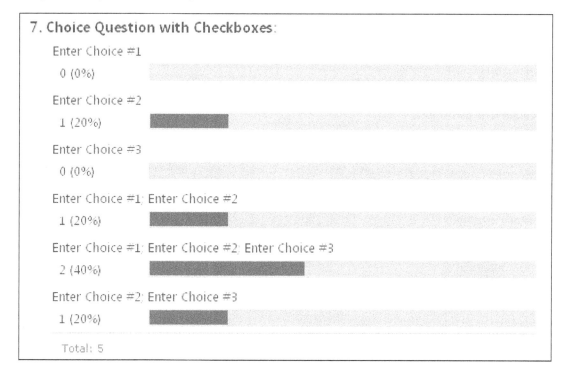

Choice Question with Checkboxes:

☑ Enter Choice #1
☐ Enter Choice #2
☑ Enter Choice #3

Graphical Response Summary

7. Choice Question with Checkboxes:

Enter Choice #1
0 (0%)

Enter Choice #2
1 (20%)

Enter Choice #3
0 (0%)

Enter Choice #1; Enter Choice #2
1 (20%)

Enter Choice #1; Enter Choice #2; Enter Choice #3
2 (40%)

Enter Choice #2; Enter Choice #3
1 (20%)

Total: 5

Choice Question with Checkboxes (Multiple Selection) and Fill-In

Using the optional "Allow Fill-In" selection allows you to create a question that provides both pre-defined checkboxes to check along with an additional checkbox for the user to enter their own answer.

If you are going to allow the user to fill-in their own answer, using the checkboxes as shown here provides a more naturally mapped user interface (versus with the drop-down menu).

User Entry Interface

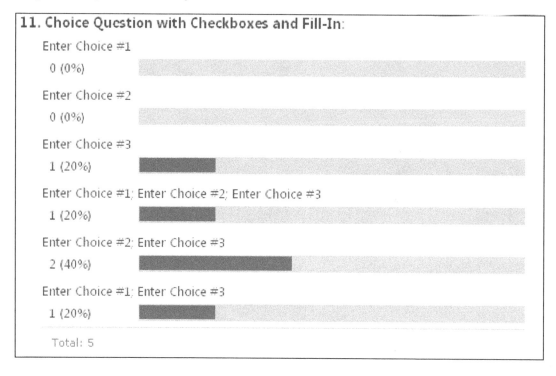

Choice Question with Checkboxes and Fill-In:

☐ Enter Choice #1
☑ Enter Choice #2
☑ Enter Choice #3
☑ Specify your own value:
   Choice #4|

Graphical Response Summary

11. Choice Question with Checkboxes and Fill-In:

Enter Choice #1
0 (0%)

Enter Choice #2
0 (0%)

Enter Choice #3
1 (20%)

Enter Choice #1; Enter Choice #2; Enter Choice #3
1 (20%)

Enter Choice #2; Enter Choice #3
2 (40%)

Enter Choice #1; Enter Choice #3
1 (20%)

Total: 5

Rating Scale Question

A Rating Scale question involves one or more sub-questions (or items) that need to be ranked in some sort of fashion. The scale of numbers is configurable as well as the rating text. There is an option to include or not include a not applicable (N/A) column. The text for the N/A column is also configurable - other examples include "I don't know" and "Prefer not to answer".

User Entry Interface

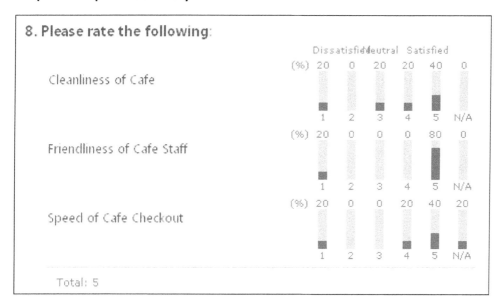

Graphical Response Summary

Branching Questions

Survey questions in SharePoint 2013 have branching logic capabilities. You may direct the user to different sets of questions based on their answer to the branching question. It sounds like you can direct the user all over the place but really you are presenting an additional set of questions because they answered in a certain way. I like to think about it as "follow-up" questions.

In this example, if the user answers Yes to the branching question and clicks next:

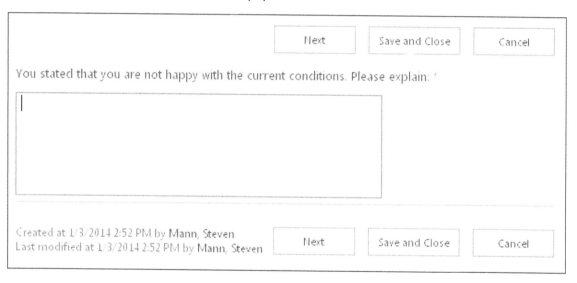

They are directed to one or more follow-up questions:

After the follow-up question(s) is complete, the survey continues:

Choice Question with Checkboxes and Fill-In:

☐ Enter Choice #1
☐ Enter Choice #2
☐ Enter Choice #3
☐ Specify your own value:

Created at 1/3/2014 2:52 PM by Mann, Steven
Last modified at 1/3/2014 2:54 PM by Mann, Steven

Finish   Cancel

When the user answers No in the example and clicks Next:

Question for Branching:

○ Yes
⊙ No

Next   Save and Close   Cancel

The survey does not present the follow-up question and continues onto the configured next question in the survey:

	Finish	Cancel

Choice Question with Checkboxes and Fill-In:

☐ Enter Choice #1

☐ Enter Choice #2

☐ Enter Choice #3

☐ Specify your own value:

[   ]

Created at 1/3/2014 2:52 PM by Mann, Steven
Last modified at 1/3/2014 2:54 PM by Mann, Steven

Finish	Cancel

Adding a Survey App to Your Site

From the settings menu (gear) select Site contents:

The Site Contents for your site appears.

On the Site Contents page, click on add an app:

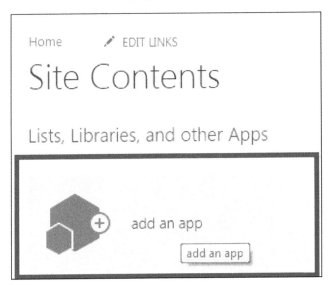

Instead of going to Site Contents first, you could simply select Add an app right from the settings (gear) menu:

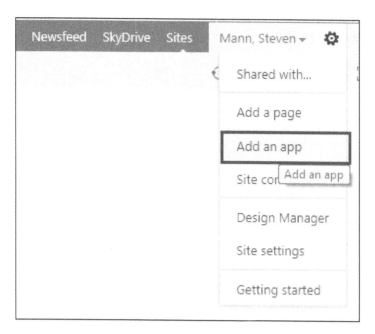

Either way, the apps page appears. Find the Survey app and click on the icon:

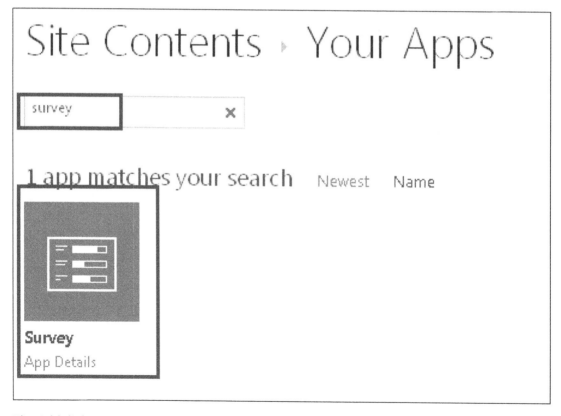

The Add dialog appears:

It is not recommended to click on Advanced Options until you become a pro and are ready to create your questions right away.

Enter a name for your survey and click Create:

A blank survey list is created:

Click on the Survey icon to open the Survey Overview page:

Office Workplace Survey

Survey Name:	Office Workplace Survey
Survey Description:	
Time Created:	1/3/2014 8:58 AM
Number of Responses:	0

▣ Show a graphical summary of responses
▣ Show all responses

Adding Survey Questions

From your survey overview page, click on the Settings menu and then select Add Questions:

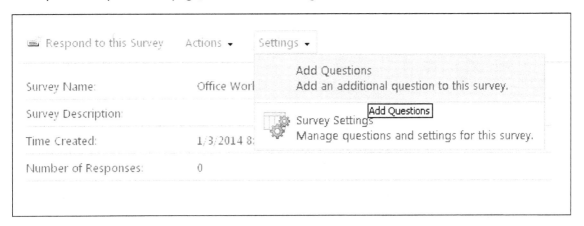

The New Question wizard appears:

Settings ▸ New Question ⓘ

Question and Type

Type your question and select the type of answer.

Question:

Type your question here...

The type of answer to this question is:

○ Single line of text
○ Multiple lines of text
⦿ Choice (menu to choose from)
○ Rating Scale (a matrix of choices or a Likert scale)
○ Number (1, 1.0, 100)
○ Currency ($, ¥, €)
○ Date and Time
○ Lookup (information already on this site)
○ Yes/No (check box)
○ Person or Group
○ Page Separator (inserts a page break into your survey)

It is called a wizard since you can create the first question and then continue on to create additional questions until you click Finish.

Creating a Free Form Single Entry Question

What is your favorite color?

Blue|

A free form single entry may be used to ask a question that may have many possible answers but not finite enough to provide choices. This is where you want the user to enter whatever they feel without being constrained to a list of choices.

Create this type of question by entering the question in the Question box (including punctuation) and then selecting Single line of text as the type of answer:

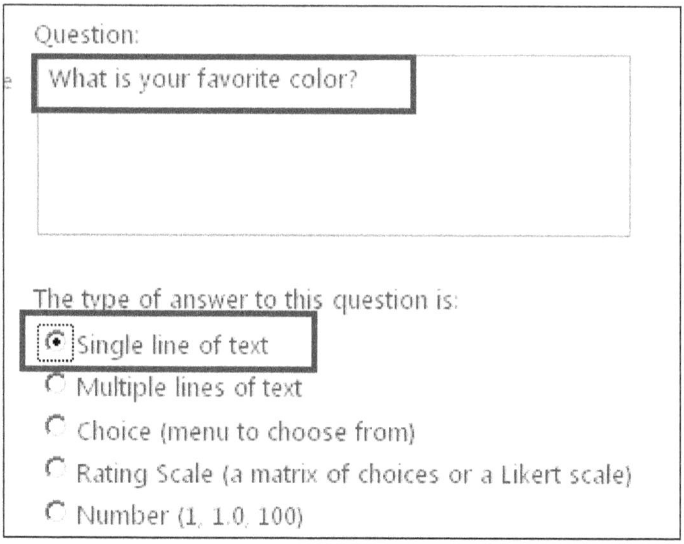

Question:

What is your favorite color?

The type of answer to this question is:

⊙ Single line of text
○ Multiple lines of text
○ Choice (menu to choose from)
○ Rating Scale (a matrix of choices or a Likert scale)
○ Number (1, 1.0, 100)

Optionally require this question to be answered:

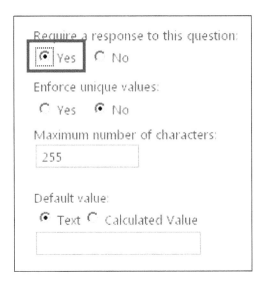

Then click the Next Question button to enter the next question in the survey:

Creating a Free Form Multiple Line Question

Please describe your main responsibilities: *

I am involved in creating solutions on our intranet that runs on
SharePoint 2013.

A free form multiple line entry should be used when you would like the user to describe an issue
or problem, provide a relatively longer (than the single line) explanation , expand on comments,
or provide recommendations/suggestions.

To create this type of question interface, enter the question in the Question box and select
Multiple lines of text as the type of answer:

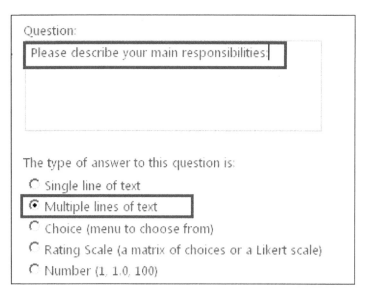

Optionally require this question to be answered. Enter the number of lines for editing. Six is the
default but you may feel you need more or less for the question being asked. Multiple line text
boxes in SharePoint have rich text capabilities but for surveys Plain text should suffice unless you
need to user to insert pictures or hyperlinks (which doesn't seem to be the norm in surveys but
the option is there if needed).

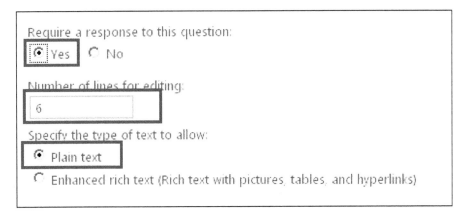

Once again click Next Question to save this one and create the next one:

Creating a Choice Question as Drop-Down

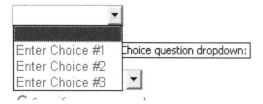

A choice question allows you to enter specific choices in which the user may select as the answer. For the drop-down type, the choices appear in a drop-down list. This type of answer interface is good for questions that may have several possible selections (5-10).

To create this type of answer interface, enter the question in the Question box and then select Choice:

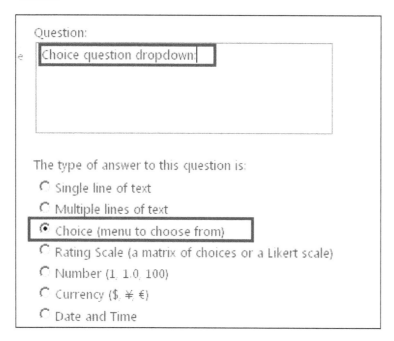

Optionally require this question to be answered and then enter the choices available in the choice text box. Select the Drop-Down Menu as the display choice:

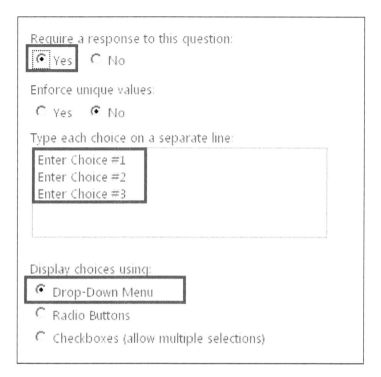

Optionally allow fill-in choices (see Planning section for example):

Creating a Choice Question as Options (Radio Buttons)

Choice Question as Options:

    ◯ Enter Choice #1
    ⦿ Enter Choice #2
    ◯ Enter Choice #3

For the Options type of choice question, the available answers to the question are presented as radio buttons in which only one may be selected. This is similar to the drop-down menu however, the user can see all options available without having the look inside the drop-down.

To create this type of question, enter the question into the Question box and select Choice as the type of answer:

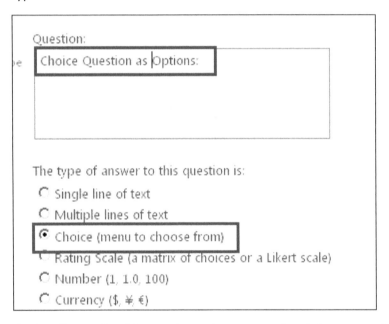

Optionally require this question to be answered and then enter the choices available in the choice text box. Select Radio Buttons as the display choice:

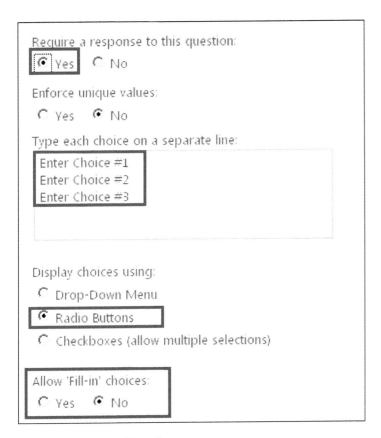

Optionally allow Fill-In choices.

Creating a Choice Question with Checkboxes (Multiple Selection)

Choice Question with Checkboxes: *

☑ Enter Choice #1
☐ Enter Choice #2
☑ Enter Choice #3

For the Checkboxes type of choice question, the available answers to the question are presented as checkboxes in which the user may select one or more answers.

To create this type of question, enter the question text including punctuation into the Question text box and select Choice as the type of answer:

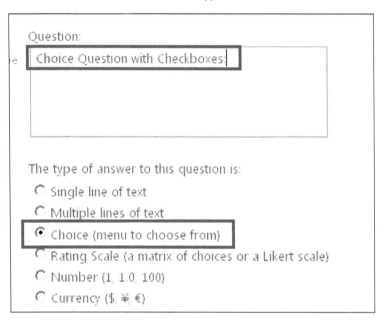

Optionally require this question to be answered and then enter the choices available in the choice text box. Select Checkboxes (allow multuple selections) as the display choice:

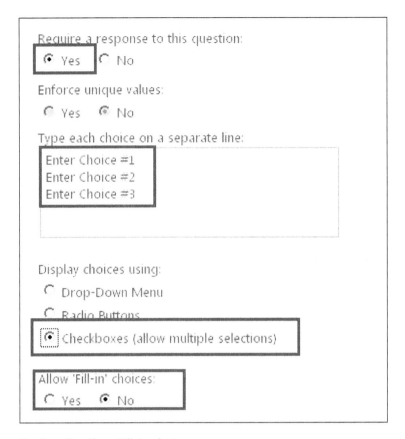

Optionally allow Fill-In choices.

Creating a Rating Scale Question

Please rate the following:	Dissatisfied		Neutral		Satisfied	
	1	2	3	4	5	N/A
Cleanliness of Cafe	○	○	○	○	◉	○
Friendliness of Cafe Staff	○	○	○	◉	○	○
Speed of Cafe Checkout	○	◉	○	○	○	○

A Rating Scale question involves one or more sub-questions (or items) that need to be ranked in some sort of fashion. The scale of numbers is configurable as well as the rating text. There is an option to include or not include a not applicable (N/A) column.

To create this type of question and answering system, first enter instructions into the Question text box and select Rating Scale as the type of answer:

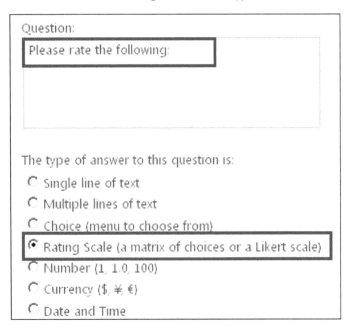

Type in each item you wish to be rated into the sub-question text box:

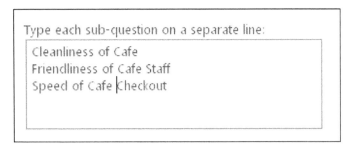

Select a number (scale) for the Number Range (usually 1-5 or 1-10 provide the best insight):

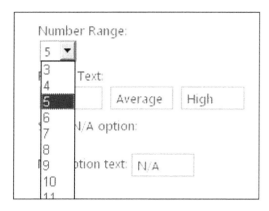

Modify the Range Text based on what is being rated:

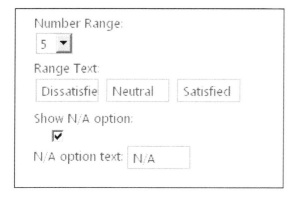

Optionally show an "N/A" option and enter the text to display. Other examples include "I don't know" and "Prefer not to answer".

Creating a Branching Question

Question:

Question for Branching:

The type of answer to this question is:

○ Single line of text
○ Multiple lines of text
● Choice (menu to choose from)
○ Rating Scale (a matrix of choices or a Likert scale)
○ Number (1, 1.0, 100)

Require a response to this question:

● Yes   ○ No

Enforce unique values:

○ Yes   ● No

Type each choice on a separate line:

Yes
No

Creating a Follow-Up Question for Branching

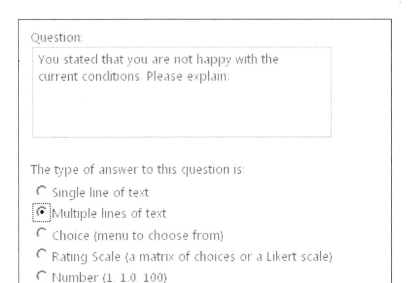

Click Finish when you have completed entering all survey questions. The list settings page appears.

Reordering Questions

Many times, especially when using branching and page separators, you need to change the ordering of the survey questions. This can be easily done in the survey list settings by clicking the Change the order of the questions link at the bottom of the question section:

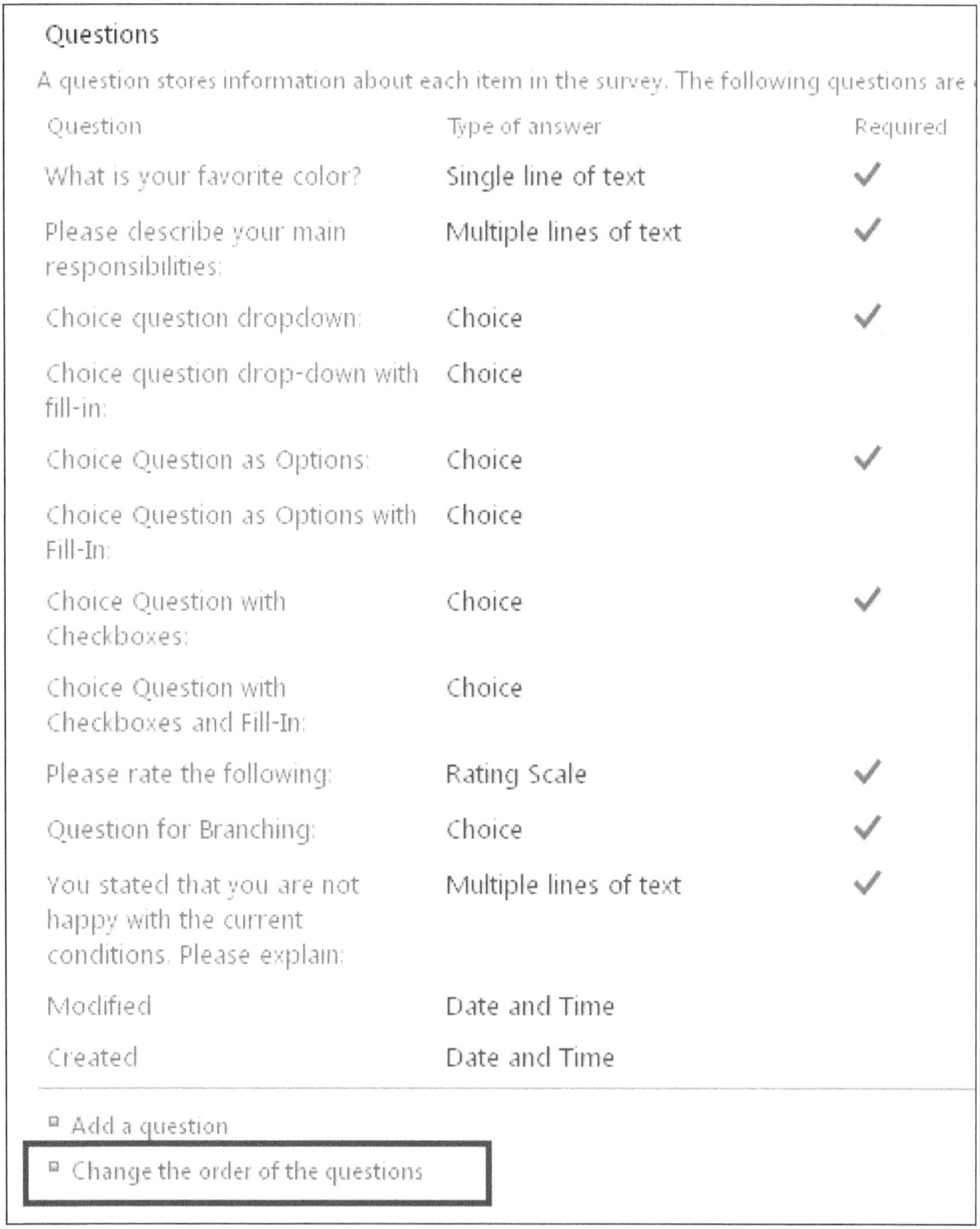

Questions

A question stores information about each item in the survey. The following questions are

Question	Type of answer	Required
What is your favorite color?	Single line of text	✓
Please describe your main responsibilities:	Multiple lines of text	✓
Choice question dropdown:	Choice	✓
Choice question drop-down with fill-in:	Choice	
Choice Question as Options:	Choice	✓
Choice Question as Options with Fill-In:	Choice	
Choice Question with Checkboxes:	Choice	✓
Choice Question with Checkboxes and Fill-In:	Choice	
Please rate the following:	Rating Scale	✓
Question for Branching:	Choice	✓
You stated that you are not happy with the current conditions. Please explain:	Multiple lines of text	✓
Modified	Date and Time	
Created	Date and Time	

▫ Add a question

▫ Change the order of the questions

The Change Column Ordering page appears:

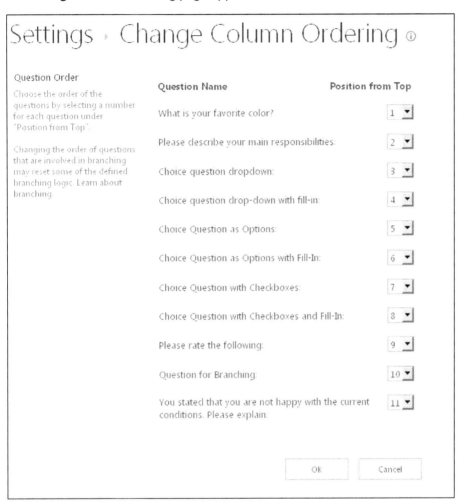

Use the Position from Top drop-down menus to change the order number for the questions:

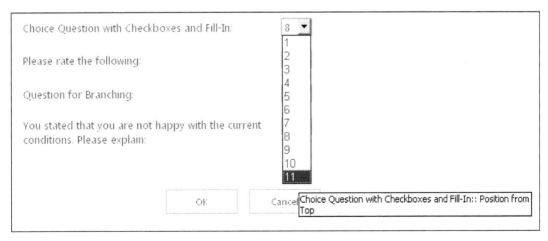

The questions are reordered in place on the page. Click OK when complete:

Please rate the following:	8 ▼
Question for Branching:	9 ▼
You stated that you are not happy with the current conditions. Please explain:	10 ▼
Choice Question with Checkboxes and Fill-In:	11 ▼

OK	Cancel

Configuring Branching Questions

The Edit Question page appears:

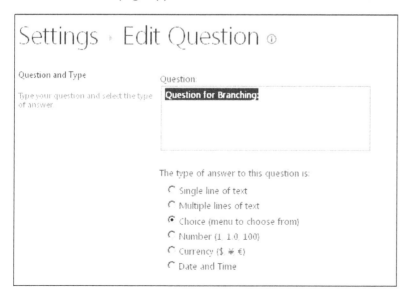

Scroll down to the Branching section. Change the Yes Jump To selection to the "You stated that...":

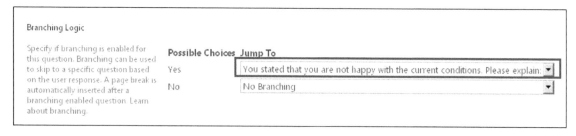

Change the No Jump To selection to "Choice Question with Checkboxes and Fill-In":

Possible Choices	Jump To
Yes	You stated that you are not happy with the current conditions. Please explain: ▼
No	Choice Question with Checkboxes and Fill-In: ▼

Click OK.

As shown in the Planning section of this guide, here is the resultant flow of the branching. Answering Yes to the branching question results in the follow-up question being displayed. After the follow-up question is answered, the survey continues with the Choice Question.

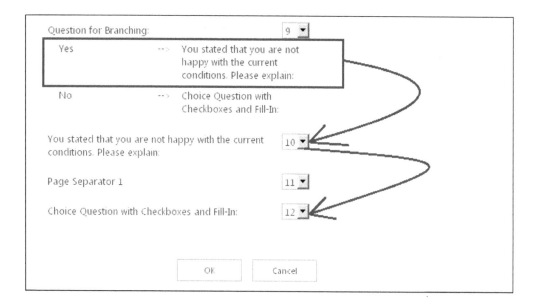

Answering No to the branching question essentially skips the follow-up question (or questions) and the survey continues past to the Choice Question:

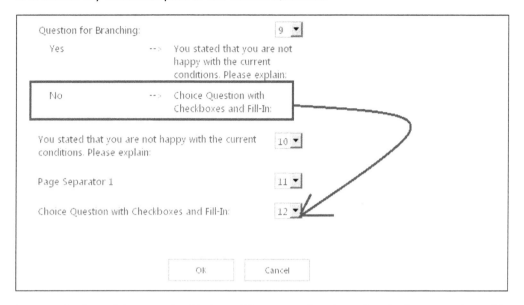

You need a Page Separator in this branching example otherwise the last question will appear with the follow-up branch question. Adding a page separator is shown in the next section.

Adding a Page Separator

Typically surveys contain "pages" of questions. This is particularly useful when using branching. You may add a page separator after each question or set of questions. To add a page separator, in the survey list settings, click on the Add a question link:

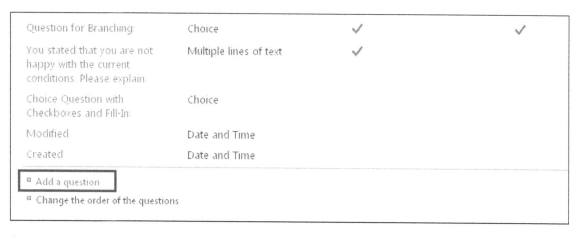

Enter Page Separator as the Question text and select Page Separator as the type of answer:

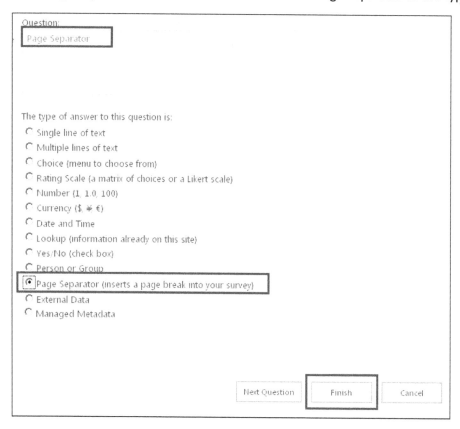

Click Finish.

Click on the Change the order of the questions link as previously discussed in the Reordering Questions section. Move the Page Separator in between the follow-up question and the last question:

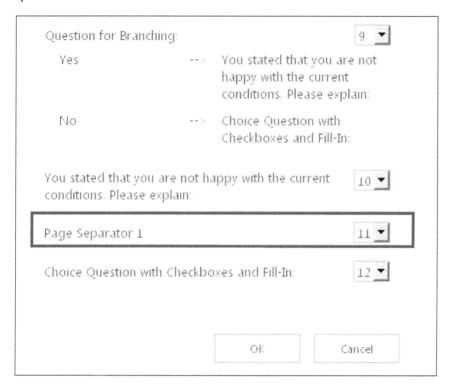

You need the separation in the branching example otherwise the last question will appear with the follow-up branch question.

The Page Separator insures that only the follow-up question is displayed and presents the Next button to continue in the survey:

Configuring Survey Options

There are several locations in which you may configure options that affect the behavior and use of a survey. This section describes the various options available.

To configure these options, navigate to your survey and select Survey Settings from the Settings menu:

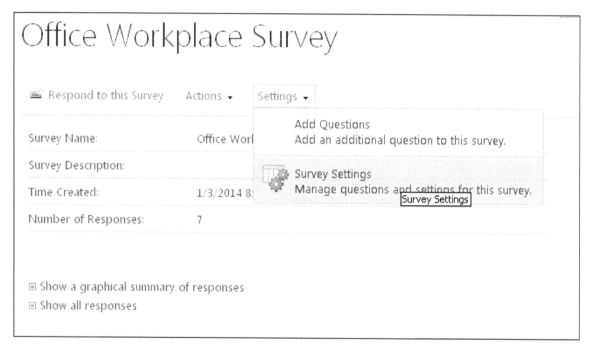

Your survey (list) settings page appears:

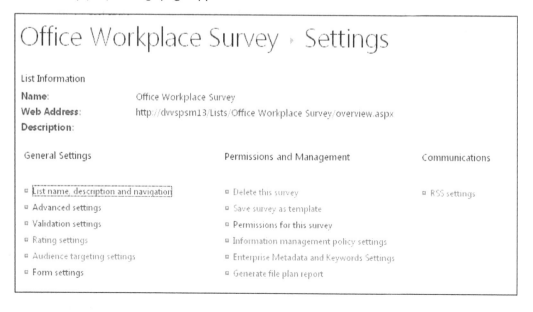

Showing Users' Names

By default the users' names are shown and recorded in the responses to the survey, however, you may change this setting such that the users' name is not shown by clicking the List name, description and navigation link:

Change the option and click Save:

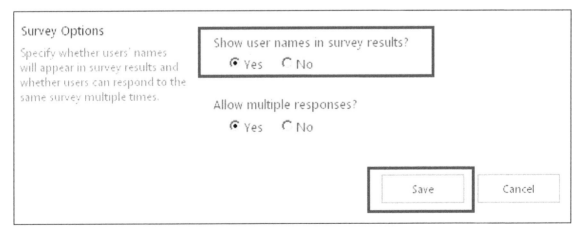

When viewing the responses, the user's name for each response is "starred" out:

View Response		Created By	Modified	Completed
View Response #5	...	...	Yesterday at 2:58 PM	Yes
View Response #6	...	...	Yesterday at 6:23 PM	Yes
View Response #7	...	...	Yesterday at 6:27 PM	Yes
View Response #8	...	...	Yesterday at 6:30 PM	Yes
View Response #9	...	...	Yesterday at 6:33 PM	No
View Response #10	...	...	Yesterday at 6:33 PM	No
View Response #11	...	...	Yesterday at 6:34 PM	Yes

Allowing Multiple Responses

By default a user may only respond to a survey once. To allow multiple responses click on the List name, description and navigation link:

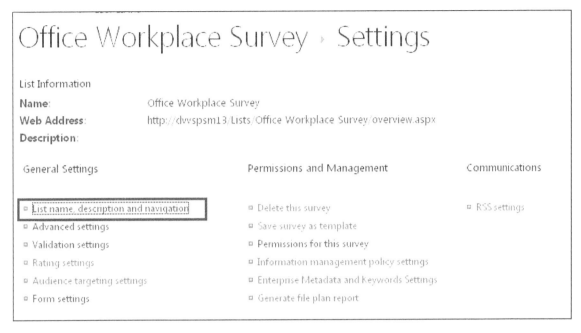

Change the option and click Save:

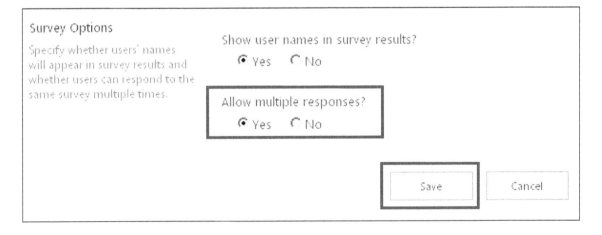

Configuring Item-Level Permissions

A major concern of surveys is who can see the responses and who is allowed to edit responses. Luckily in SharePoint 2013 each list as Item-level Permission settings. This is accessed from the Advanced settings link:

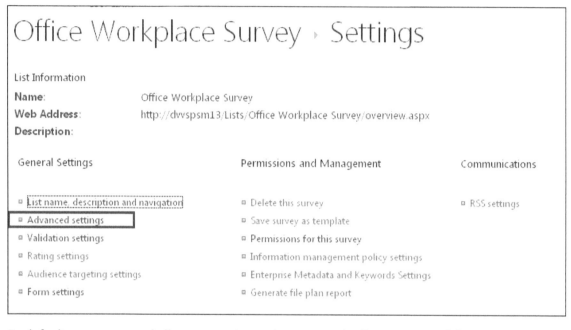

By default users may read all responses but only create and edit responses of their own:

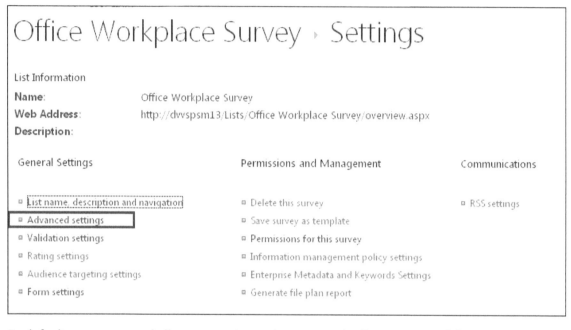

The default Create and Edit access seems appropriate, however, you may not want everyone to see all of the responses. So for the Read access setting, you may want to change the option to "Read responses that were created by the user".

Click OK on the Advanced Settings screen to save any changes.

Removing Survey Responses from Search Results

Even though search results are security trimmed, people with access to the survey responses will still see them appear in search results. This can be very annoying. Do you know how many times I have seen what someone selected as their entrée for a reception?

There is an option to not display the survey responses in the search results to solve this problem (if you encounter issues). This is accessed from the Advanced settings link:

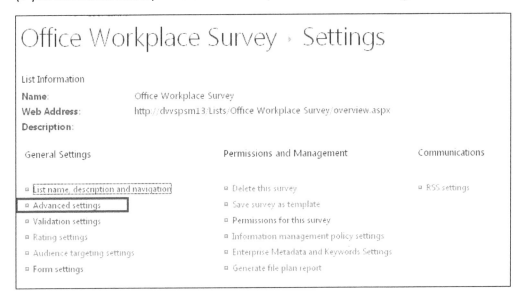

Scroll down to the Search section and change the option to No:

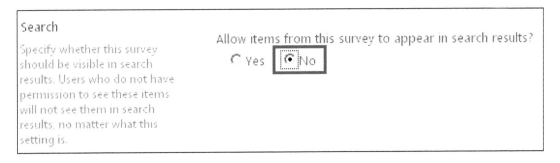

Click OK on the Advanced Settings screen to save any changes.

Survey Responses

Sending Your Survey Out for Responses

Now that you have your survey created and configured, you need people to fill out the survey. This can be easily done by sending the link to your survey to them:

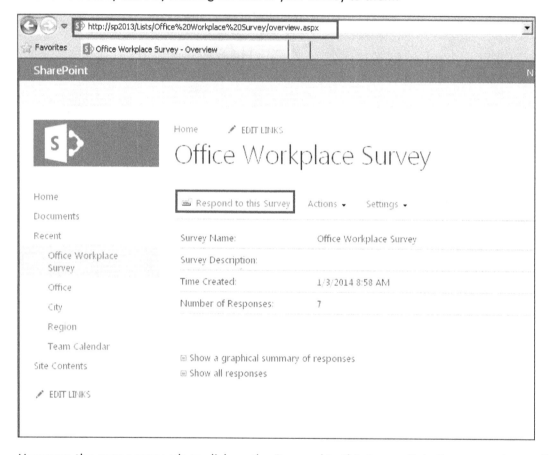

However, the user now needs to click on the Respond to this Survey link. So an even better link to send people is the response link itself. To get this link, click on the Respond to this Survey link:

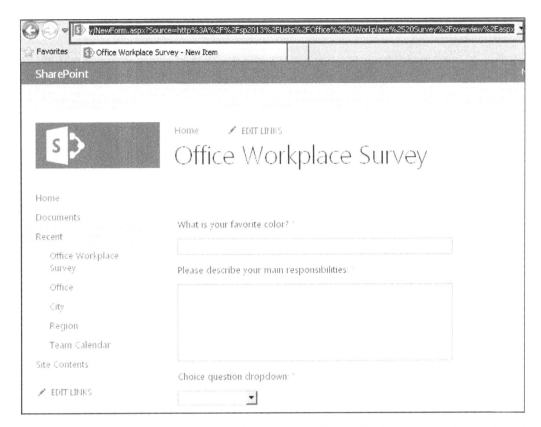

Now copy and paste the URL from the browser. This link will take the user directly into the survey; ready for answers.

When the survey is complete, the user by default will be returned to your survey overview. If you would like them to return to your home page instead (or any other location), change the ?Source= in the URL that you copy:

http://sp2013/Lists/Office%20Workplace%20Survey/NewForm.aspx**?Source=http://sp2013/**

Viewing All Responses

To see a list of all of the survey responses, navigate to your survey and either change the View using the drop-down menu or simply click the Show all responses link:

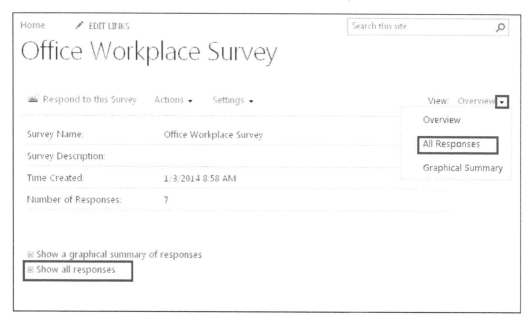

The list of responses is displayed:

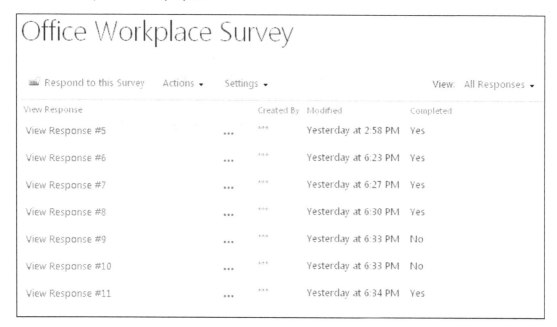

Viewing Responses in a Graphical Summary

To see the survey responses in an enlightening graphical summary, navigate to your survey and either change the View using the drop-down menu or simply click the Show a graphical summary of responses link:

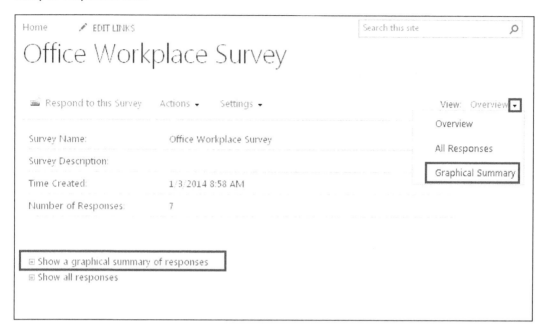

The Graphical Summary view of responses is displayed:

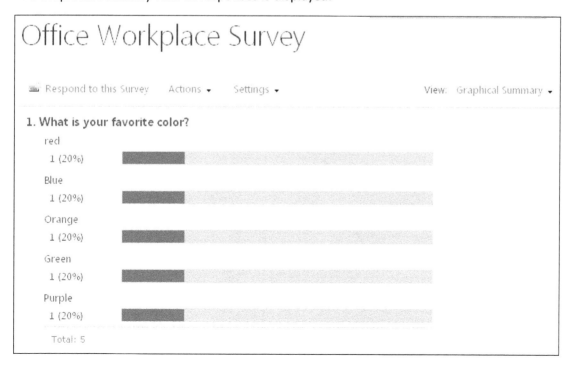

About the Author

Steve Mann was born and raised in Philadelphia, Pennsylvania, where he still resides. He is an Enterprise Application Engineer for Morgan Lewis and has over 20 years of professional experience. He has authored and co-authored several books related to collaboration technology. Steve graduated Drexel University in 1993.

Steve's blog site can be found at: www.SteveTheManMann.com

Follow Steve on Twitter @stevethemanmann